70 FUN ACTIVITIES FOR ADULTS!

Adult Activity Book

COLORING & PUZZLES

S#!T!

I'M BORED!

SAUCY SWEAR WORDS

Thank you for purchasing this adult activity book! It is filled with 70+ relaxing activities to entertain you, reduce stress and challenge your critical thinking skills with activities such as: coloring, mazes, word scrambles, crossword puzzles, word search puzzles and more. There are fun activities for all skill levels in this book from beginners to advanced. Have fun and enjoy your new activity book!

*** WARNING Please be advised ***
this book contains sexually EXPLICIT language and content. It is INTENDED for adult entertainment only and not for use by children. THE CONTENT IS NOT MEANT TO OFFEND ANYONE; HOWEVER, IT IS ALSO NOT IN ANY WAY POLITE or POLITICALLY CORRECT.

ENJOY!

Want a freebie?

Check out the end of the book to get a fun FREE gift!

Look for more Adult Activity Books

NEVER HAVE I EVER GAME

How fucking adventurous are you? Check off each item below that you have done. Each checked item is one point. Next add your total points and see how you scored!

☐ **Never have I ever done it in a public place.**

☐ **Never have I ever finished myself off after sex because I wasn't satisfied.**

☐ **Never have I ever been asked for a threesome.**

☐ **Never have I ever masturbated seeing porn**

☐ **Never have I ever looked up new sex positions on the internet.**

What's your score?_____

5 - Wow! You're amazing!
4 - Not too bad
3 - Meh. Kinda boring
2 - Yikes. Not that great
1 - Time to live a little more!

Sexy Sudoku 1

Damn this shit is hard! Try to kick this puzzles ass before it kicks yours!

	6			3			8	
3			7		8			9
2	8		6	9	5		4	7
		2	3		1	4		
	5		9		6		1	
		8	5		2	9		
1	3		4	2	7		9	8
5			8		9			1
	9			5			2	

Motherfucking Maze 1

Try to solve this hard ass maze! Start from the top and figure out how to get the fuck out of this shit!

Odd One Out 1

Damn this shit is hard! Try to find the one that's fucking different.

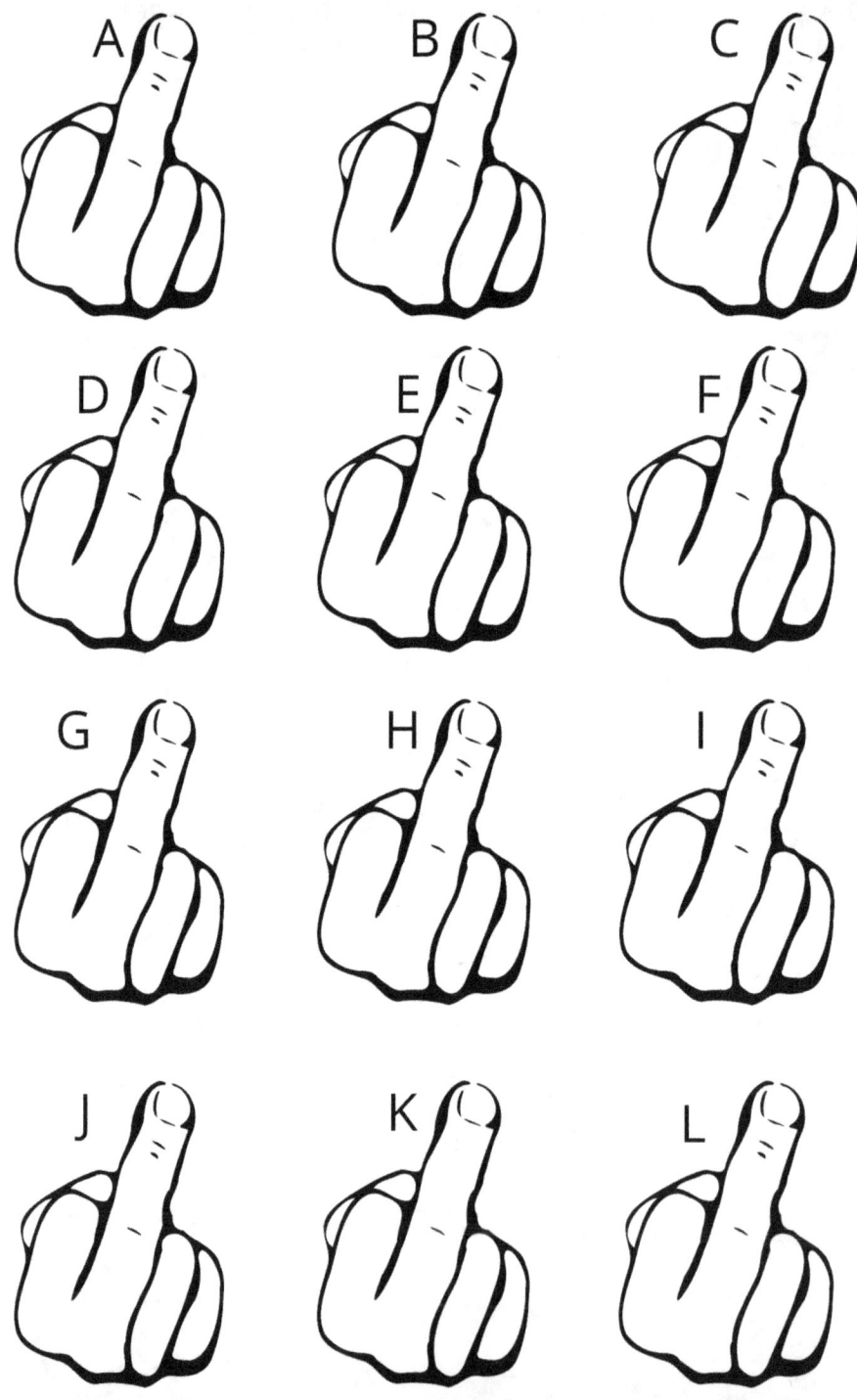

Sexy Sudoku 2

Damn this shit is hard! Try to kick this puzzles ass before it kicks yours!

8			6	7	1			4
	2	1		4		7	3	
4	9		5	2	3		6	1
	3						8	
2		9				1		7
	1	6	2		8	3	4	
1								3
	4	5		9		2	7	
	7						1	

WTF! Word Search 2

Solve this damn puzzle...if you can.

Top 20 Popular British Swear Words

```
P  J  G  C  M  I  Z  X  R  C  W  E  N  R  Z  C  O  A  U  M
S  K  C  T  V  J  K  N  C  F  K  F  P  A  X  T  T  C  D  F
H  D  A  M  N  M  X  U  D  Z  J  R  N  Y  U  M  F  A  W  Q
I  P  S  D  X  Z  F  H  G  C  H  E  V  P  Z  L  R  W  I  C
T  U  D  X  R  F  D  X  X  R  L  G  I  R  U  N  N  Q  L  U
R  Q  X  F  L  A  V  R  O  O  A  G  P  R  Y  S  T  M  X  D
Z  E  X  G  B  J  T  C  H  F  O  U  T  E  L  X  S  B  R  I
N  P  Q  S  T  K  R  S  R  Y  T  B  H  N  X  D  B  Y  T  L
X  F  Y  G  Q  N  R  Q  A  Z  U  C  R  V  Z  Y  Q  C  B  Z
V  W  S  F  S  A  U  K  P  B  U  P  L  K  R  M  Y  O  K  L
X  D  W  M  P  O  J  C  J  O  O  B  V  T  Y  S  N  D  W  A
C  G  V  M  X  J  K  X  D  J  K  H  O  U  C  D  J  P  S  A
R  E  C  E  V  P  E  C  V  O  C  P  C  L  F  S  O  S  G  X
A  W  P  W  R  W  J  X  I  Q  X  U  G  S  L  C  H  O  F  J
P  B  I  T  C  H  S  G  Z  D  C  P  O  Z  A  O  I  U  L  Q
N  J  E  O  L  J  H  M  E  N  I  D  D  X  L  A  C  U  K  B
O  H  C  J  N  I  R  T  T  S  P  G  S  E  Q  K  S  K  E  W
B  K  B  X  Y  N  S  C  S  I  P  V  C  S  H  R  A  S  S  V
O  G  T  O  Y  K  T  L  Y  S  R  F  L  Q  M  G  O  G  B  P
O  K  H  F  I  A  L  L  E  J  W  K  N  E  S  N  G  C  R  J
```

FUCK	SHIT	BLOODY
PISS	BITCH	CRAP
COCK	CUNT	DAMN
DICK	BASTARD	BUGGER
FAG	PUSSY	BOLLOCKS
SLUT	ARSHOLE	DARN
ASSHOLE	DOUCHE	

Dirty Dot to Dot

What the fuck is this? Connect the dots and solve the puzzle

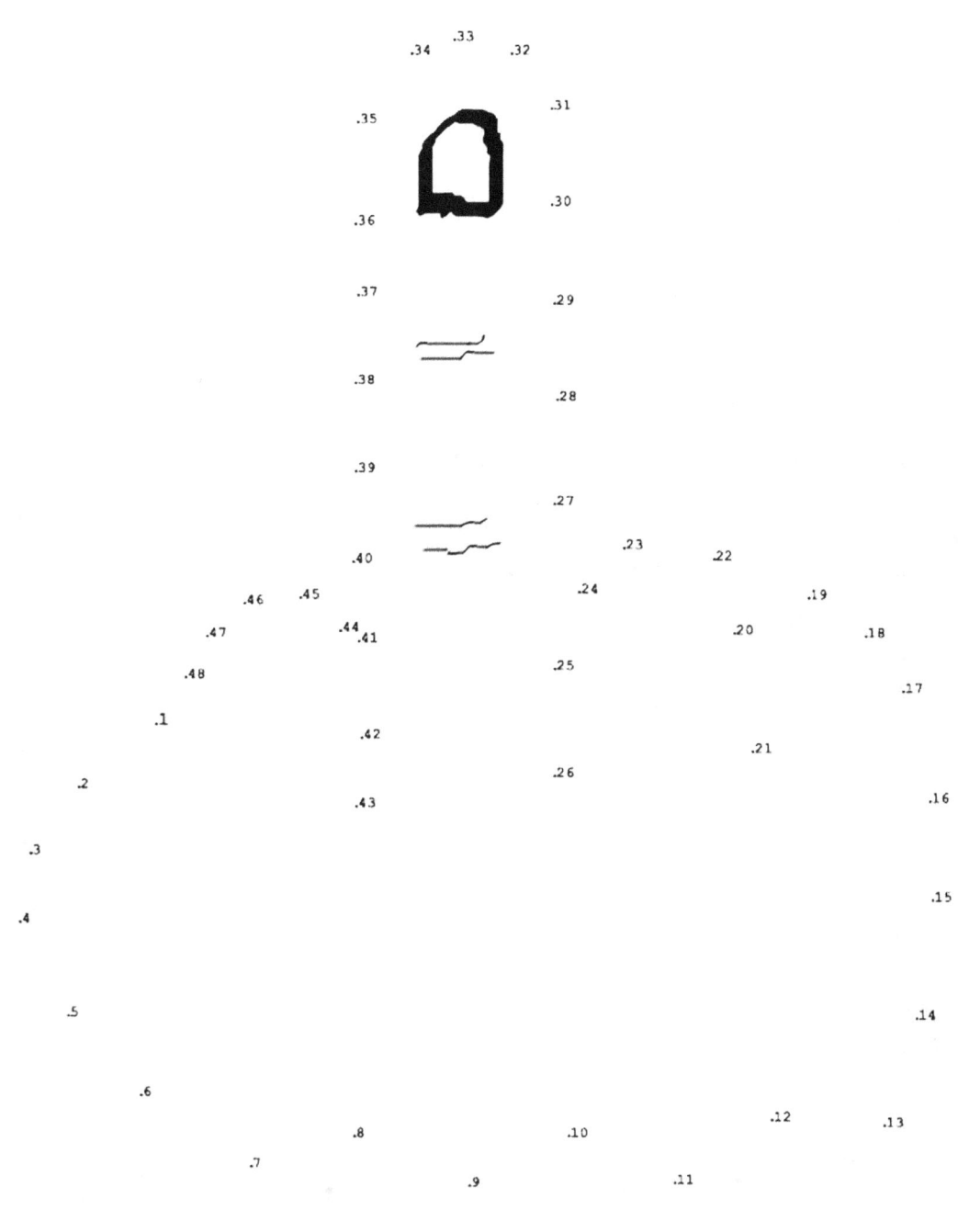

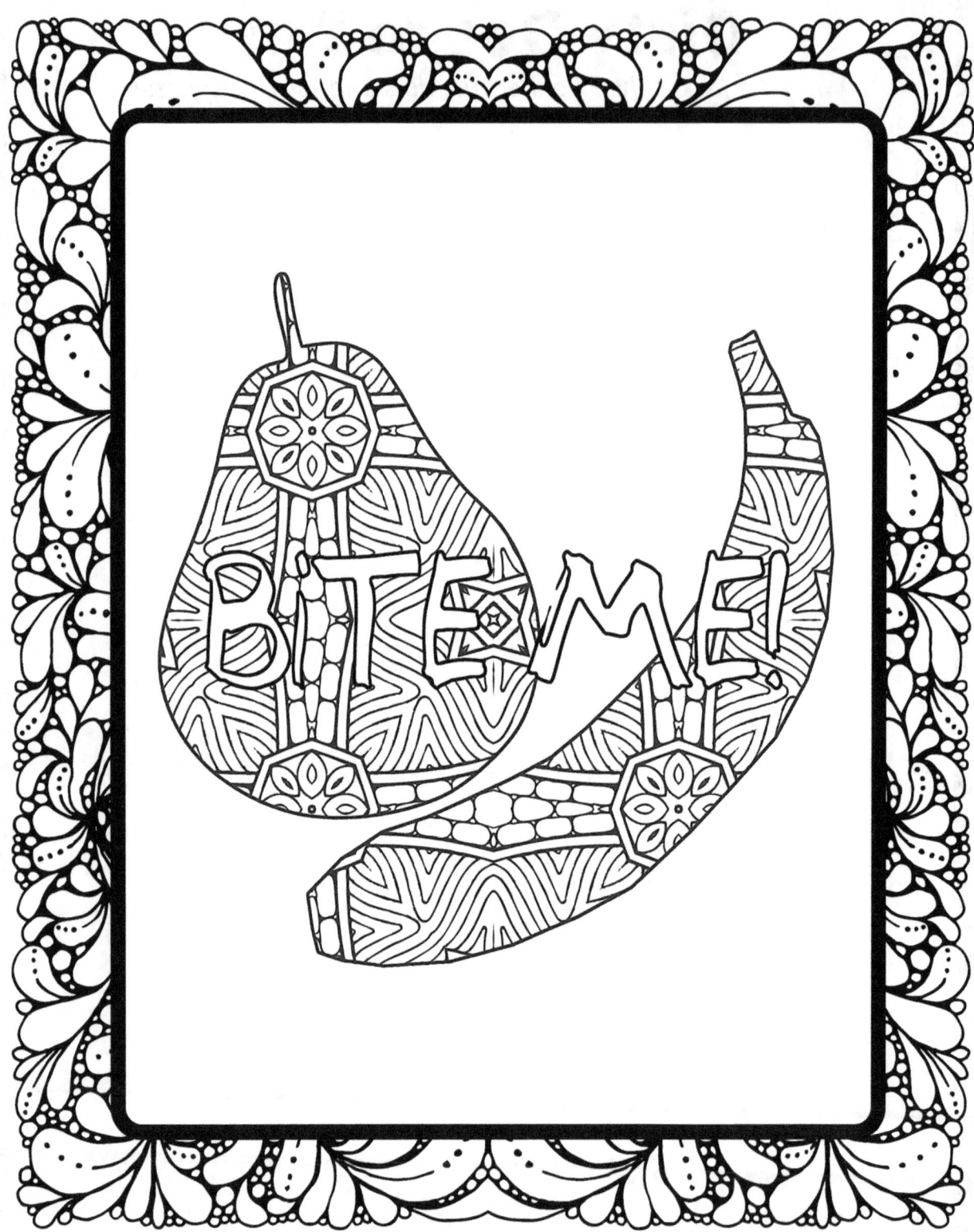

TRUE OR FALSE

A pig's penis is shaped
like a corkscrew

Circle the answer below

T   F

Kickass Kakuro 1

The rules of Kakuro are fucking simple - place the damn numbers 1 to 9 into the puzzle grid so that each continuous horizontal or vertical run of empty squares adds up to the value to the left of it or above it respectively. This value is shown either to the right or below a diagonal line. Got it? Now go and solve this shit!

Sexy Sudoku 3

Damn this shit is hard! Try to kick this puzzles ass before it kicks yours!

4	6		7	3	5		8	2
2				6				1
		3		1		6		
6				4				3
7	1	5	3		2	4	6	8
3				7				5
		2		5		1		
1				2				7
9	4		1	8	3		2	6

OMG **Odd One Out 3**

Damn this shit is hard! Try to find the one that's fucking different.

A B C

D E F

G H I

J K L

NEVER HAVE I EVER GAME

How fucking adventurous are you? Check off each item below that you have done. Each checked item is one point. Next add your total points and see how you scored!

☐ **Never have I ever tried having sex on video call.**

☐ **Never have I ever kissed someone of the same s*x.**

☐ **Never have I ever hit on someone while on a date with someone else.**

☐ **Never have I ever used an old picture of myself on a dating site.**

☐ **Never have I ever made out in the toilet.**

What's your score?_____

5 - Wow! You're amazing!
4 - Not too bad
3 - Meh. Kinda boring
2 - Yikes. Not that great
1 - Time to live a little more!

Finish the Fucking Picture 1

Think you know what the fuck this is? Draw the other half of the picture

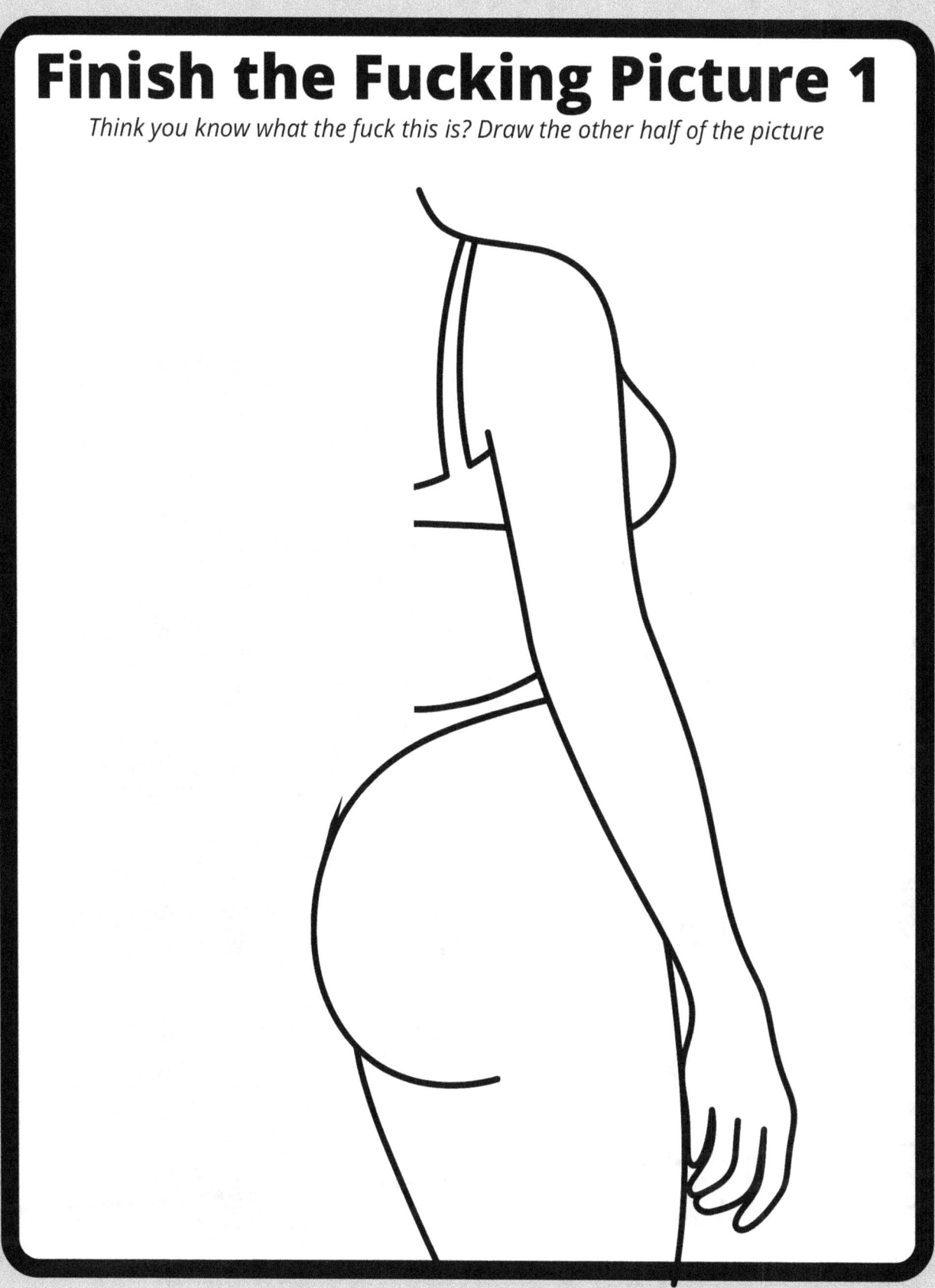

OMG Odd One Out 2

Damn this shit is hard! Try to find the one that's fucking different.

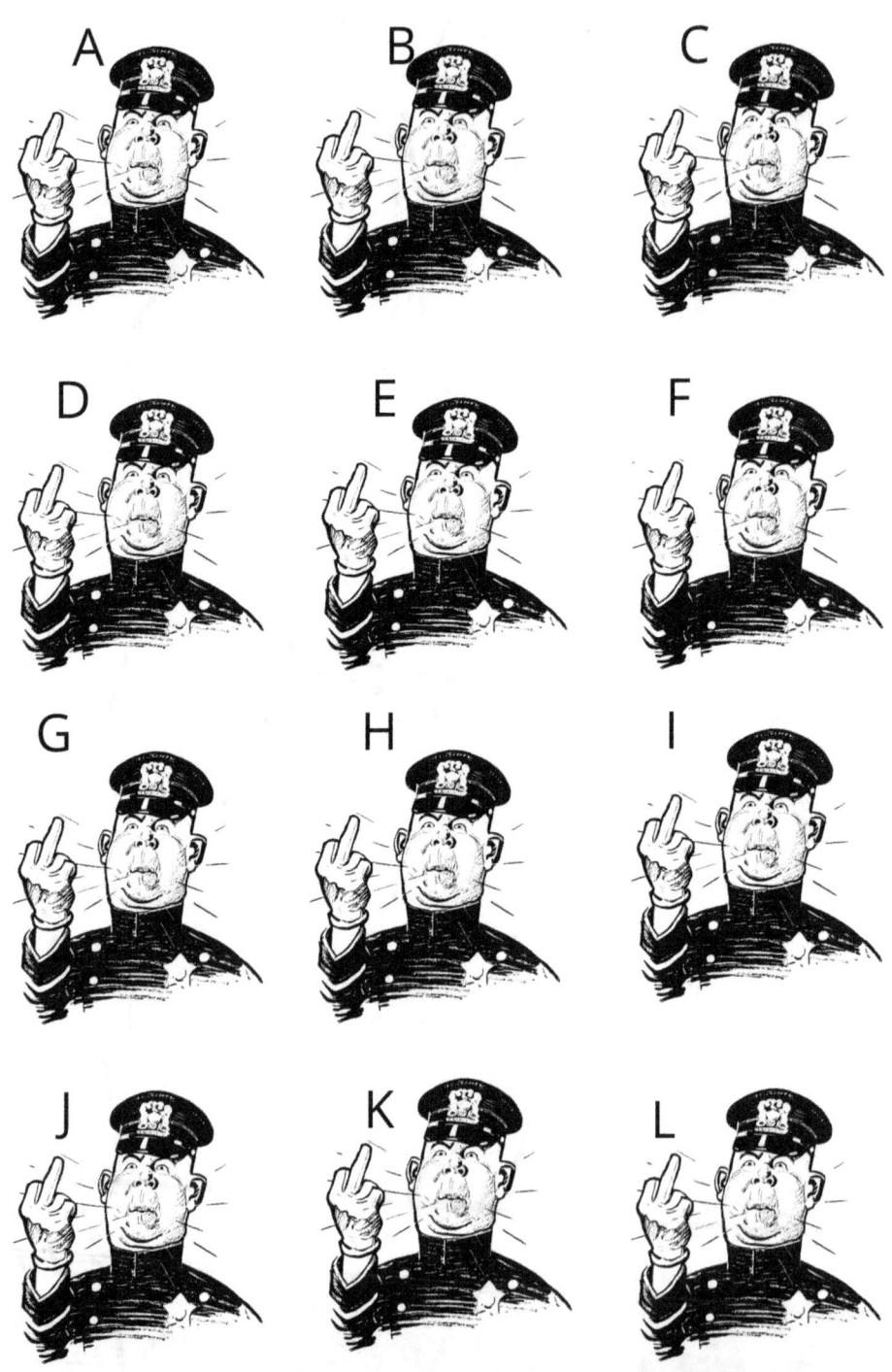

A B C

D E F

G H I

J K L

WTF! Word Search 1

Solve this damn puzzle...if you can.

Top 15 Southern Swear Words

```
S Z K Y B S X T N U D M F B G N G P S H
S Z A Z Q Z G Z K Q A O Z I W U M Z I L
W V N G D I B W A M R X H O O J V D Q Q
B Y H C T I B Y N R N U W U I J S A G P
I S M B I E Q K C U K M X W W N E Q O H
C I L Y H Y A V A A R S X N E Q K C I D
E Y S V S N V C P J Q B H N D B F Q F O
A J C S V A H K C I X E M Y M K Y Q M O
R G W S C H X M C D O S L U T O H X Q B
U F P X B N K X O U Q S C O T C V W I Q
S D O C D R L U Y B F T W H H W P F F I
V B B O I U C I Y I X H P U S S Y L K T
Z C S C G H T B U K E D A M N S S I P P
E N T K E M D V L Q U B Z A K K H A R U
F A G X V R C Z V G S I Z M S Z F W L G
K P M X A R N Y T B V Q F H W O S D S D
Q U A T A Z R O O I Z I D M E T A B D A
S E S P D Z O D R T F S J Z S U N O X X
T A F B D N X F D X S Q C B V F Q R I L
B B Y D B L U S N M X V Y I K O I P W E
```

SHIT	FUCK	DAMN
BITCH	CRAP	PISS
DICK	DARN	COCK
PUSSY	ASSHOLE	FAG
BASTARD	SLUT	DOUCHE

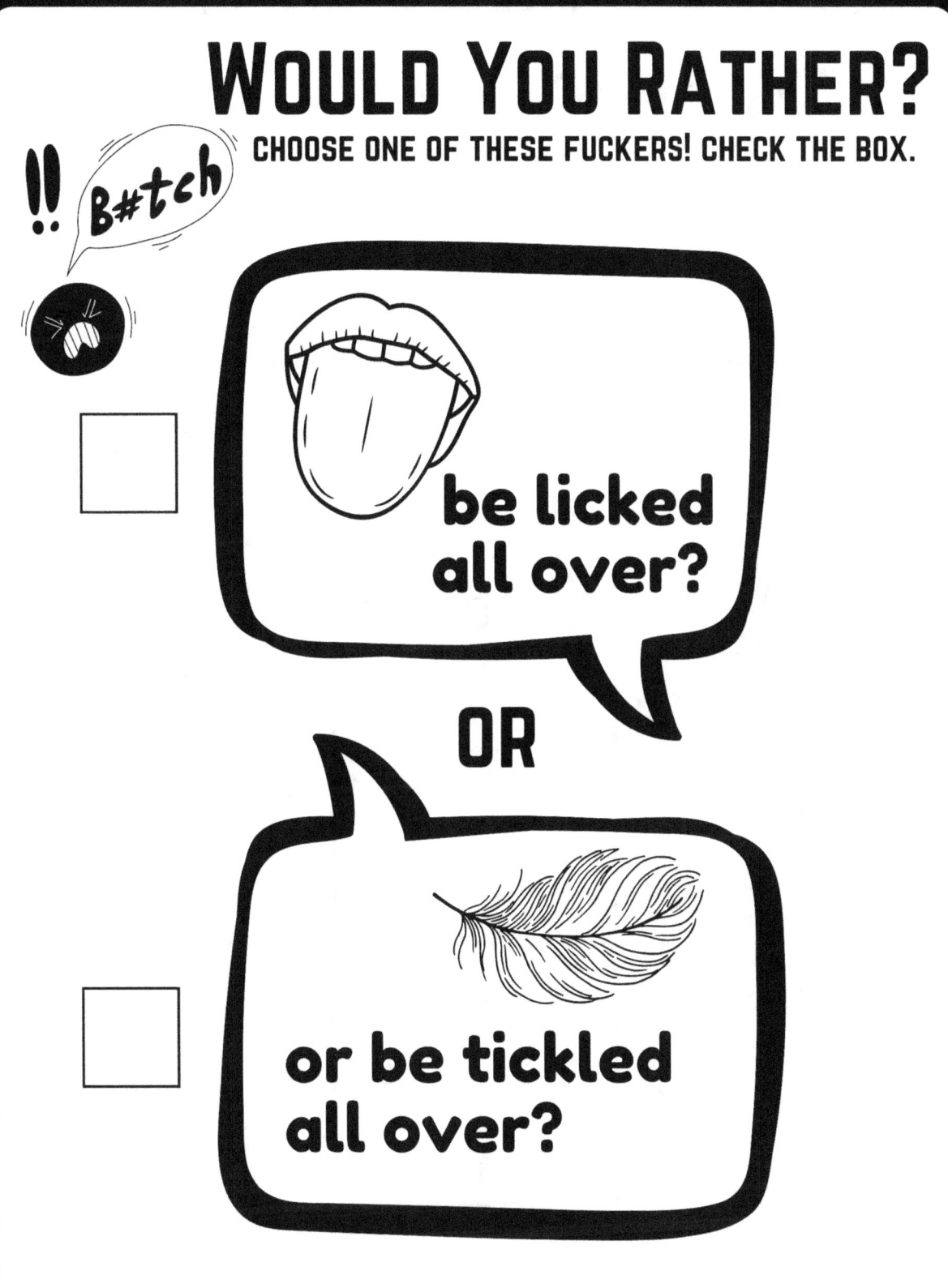

Sexy Sudoku 4

Damn this shit is hard! Try to kick this puzzles ass before it kicks yours!

				3		2	5	
3		6	4		5	8		
5	9		7	8	2		3	
	3	1				9	6	
7		9				5		8
	5	8				7	1	
	7		8	4	1		2	9
	2	3		6	1			5
	1	3		5				

WTF! Word Search 3

Solve this damn puzzle...if you can.

Feelin' Shitty

```
D  B  K  S  B  D  S  W  D  L  Q  G  P  A  V
F  D  E  C  A  F  T  I  H  S  Y  G  T  Q  C
A  L  Z  M  I  C  P  A  R  C  E  S  Z  A  Y
H  S  L  X  Y  D  I  A  Q  F  E  D  X  R  Q
G  S  Y  D  U  W  O  F  R  I  D  K  L  W  G
W  H  Y  I  P  E  K  O  T  A  S  U  I  D  A
D  I  I  P  R  L  W  T  K  Y  S  U  H  Q  S
P  T  W  S  B  O  I  S  V  I  A  Z  U  H  S
B  T  J  H  N  H  B  E  L  Y  E  F  E  D  H
I  Y  Z  I  S  T  D  F  A  D  M  B  E  V  O
L  D  L  T  A  T  C  C  R  M  A  M  E  O  L
J  U  H  M  Y  U  G  C  D  U  L  S  E  K  E
Y  L  J  C  B  B  R  G  A  M  K  H  Y  D  G
D  X  Z  W  W  V  X  K  S  D  Y  X  L  P  D
N  S  H  Z  K  G  R  Z  S  H  A  D  E  M  T
```

DOOKIE	DIPSHIT	LARDASS
LAMEASS	SHITFACED	SHITTIEST
SHITTY	CRAP	ASSHOLE
BUTTHOLE		

Cocky Crossword 1

Solve this shit ...if you can.

Random Fuckery

ACROSS
2   a person who, eloquently speaking, is such a complete and utterly disgrace to mankind
5   a party or gathering of people, with the express purpose of having sex with various partners.
6   To be doomed to misery in the near future
11 Military term for an operation in which multiple things have gone wrong
12 someone who always seems happy, even when it's not appropriate or necessary.

DOWN
1   which is an attitude of generally giving up
3   To be extremely drunk.
4   Sex only on Anniversaries, Birthdays and Christmas
6   shorter word for "fucking ugly"
7   a person who is an idiot and shows it all too well
8   feeling disinclined to do a thing, despite really knowing one ought to care about it
9   A fucklaton is the largest amount there can be of any given thing.

10 spanish for fire truck
12 Nonsense; To make no sense; Bullshit.

TRUE OR FALSE

Married men revealed that they change their underwear twice as often as single men.

Circle the answer below

T   F

WTH? Word Scramble 1

These words are all fucked up. See if you can figure this shit out.

Swear-ish Words
Please unscramble the words below

1. dnar

2. rpca

3. bllu

4. npku

5. eby leiafic

6. sith uskcs

7. ibet em

8. ejrk

9. god gneo it

10. ckrpi

11. sblal

12. uttblheo

13. sips

14. uodcch

Motherfucking Maze 3

Try to solve this hard ass maze! Start from the top and figure out how to get the fuck out of this shit!

Dirty Dot to Dot

What the fuck is this? Connect the dots and solve the puzzle

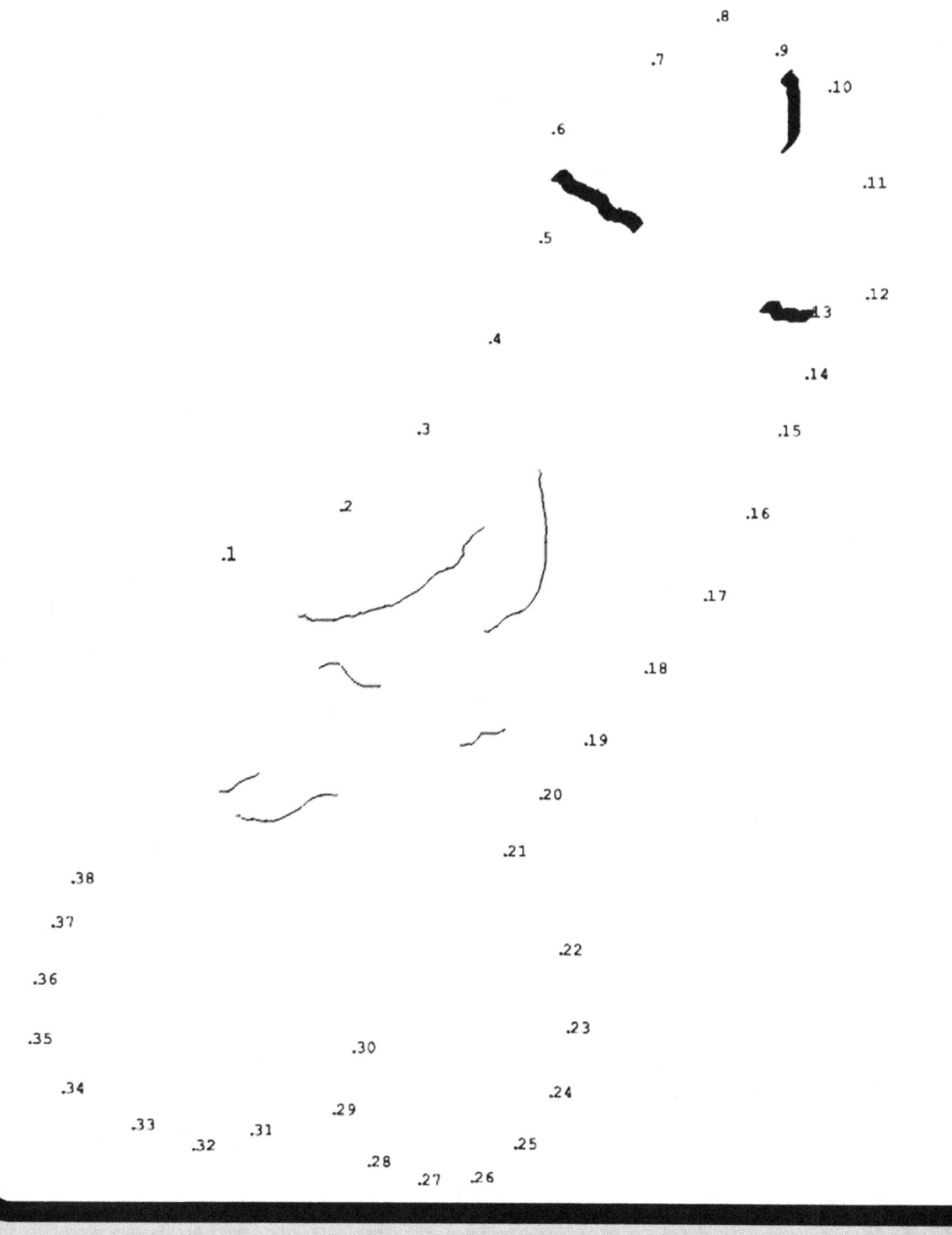

NEVER HAVE I EVER GAME

How fucking adventurous are you? Check off each item below that you have done. Each checked item is one point. Next add your total points and see how you scored!

☐ **Never have I ever peed my pants for laughing so hard.**

☐ **Never have I ever sniffed my undergarments to check if it is clean or not.**

☐ **Never have I ever forgotten to wash my hands post a pee.**

☐ **Never have I ever picked my nose in the last 24 hours.**

☐ **Never have I ever licked my arm in public to see their reactions.**

What's your score?_____

5 - Wow! You're amazing!
4 - Not too bad
3 - Meh. Kinda boring
2 - Yikes. Not that great
1 - Time to live a little more!

Crazy Ass Cryptogram 1

What the fuck is this? Can you solve the shit out of this puzzle? Find the correct letters that correspond to the letters shown below to solve the secret phrase.

A	B	C	D	E	F	G	H	I	J	K	L	M	N	O	P	Q	R	S	T	U	V	W	X	Y	Z
13	7	20	19	6	16	25	23	3	9	1	4	15	21	8	17	12	2	5	14	26	22	10	11	24	18

_ _ _ _ _   _ _ _   _ _ _ _   _ _ _ _
3   14 8 8 1   14 23 6   2 8 13 19   4 6 5 5

_ _ _ _ _ _ _ _ _   _ _ _   _   _ _ _   _   _ _ _ _
14 2 13 22 6 4 4 6 19   21 8 10   3   19 8 21   14   1 21 8 10

_ _ _ _ _   _ _ _   _ _ _ _   _   _ _
10 23 6 2 6   14 23 6   16 26 20 1   3   13 15

Sexy Sudoku 5

Damn this shit is hard! Try to kick this puzzles ass before it kicks yours!

	2	9		1		4	8	
			9		7			
3	7		5	4	8		9	2
	9	2				5	7	
8								1
	1	5				3	2	
7	8		4	3	6		5	9
			1		2			
	6	4		9		8	1	

WOULD YOU RATHER?

CHOOSE ONE OF THESE FUCKERS! CHECK THE BOX.

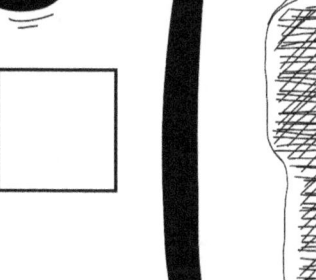
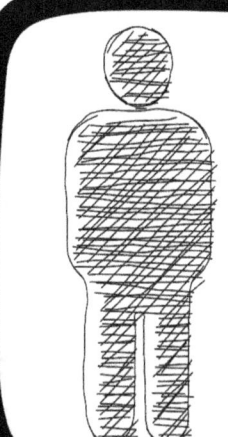

OR

WTF! Word Search 3

Solve this damn puzzle...if you can.

$#!%.

Kinda Sweary

```
D  L  B  Q  J  A  F  T  E  S  T  M  E  S  P
S  H  O  O  T  F  C  D  L  L  D  I  C  M  O
Z  F  N  J  O  P  N  L  V  E  W  Y  B  K  F
C  Z  F  S  G  E  A  R  L  W  O  W  Q  G  R
J  V  S  D  Q  B  L  R  A  H  U  X  X  G  Q
Y  I  G  O  E  P  T  O  E  D  L  V  R  C  X
P  T  B  U  J  K  C  M  H  Z  Y  E  G  X  A
O  I  L  C  U  E  E  Q  C  T  P  P  N  V  P
Y  B  T  H  V  T  K  Q  I  P  T  Y  Y  C  A
W  M  O  E  I  N  O  M  A  B  H  U  Y  D  R
T  Y  C  B  D  O  C  R  D  A  L  P  B  X  C
J  Z  D  A  X  V  C  Q  W  M  M  R  A  X  L
I  G  E  G  Y  F  F  L  V  K  N  V  S  N  L
C  P  Y  O  A  D  Y  K  X  O  F  P  T  R  U
I  U  J  E  R  K  H  E  U  B  U  P  Y  E  B
```

BITEME	PISSOFF	JERK
BUTTHOLE	BULLCRAP	DARN
IT	BLUEBALLS	DOUCHEBAG
CRAPPER	SHOOT	

Shitfaced Samurai Sudoku 3

This damn puzzle is hard! I bet you can't figure this damn thing out! Samurai sudoku puzzles consist of five overlapping sudoku grids. The standard sudoku rules apply to each 9 x 9 grid. Place digits from 1 to 9 in each empty cell. Every row, every column, and every 3 x 3 box should contain one of each digit.

Spot the Damn Difference 3

There are 5 fucking differences in the picture below. Find that shit if you can!

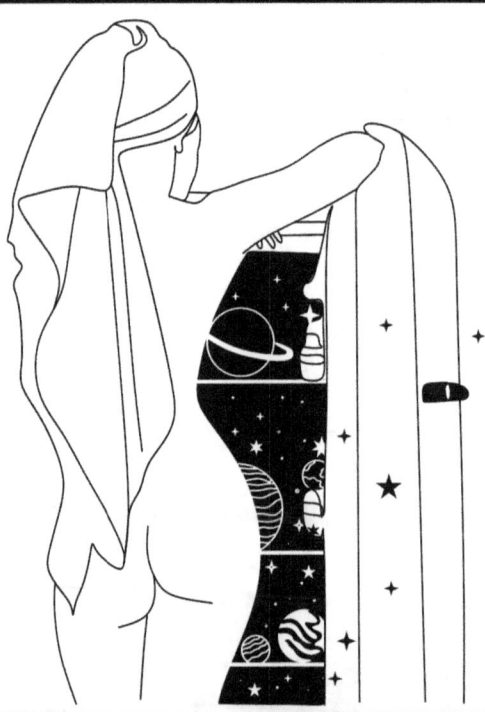

TRUE OR FALSE

48 percent of the content on the internet is pornographic

Circle the answer below

T   F

Finish the Fucking Picture 2

Think you know what the fuck this is?
Draw the other half of the picture

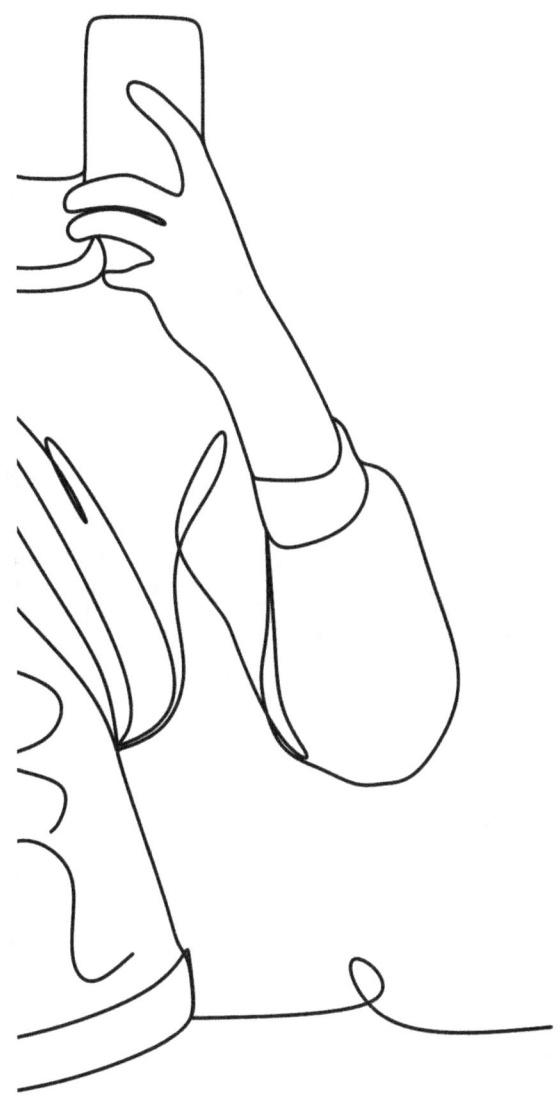

NEVER HAVE I EVER GAME

How fucking adventurous are you? Check off each item below that you have done. Each checked item is one point. Next add your total points and see how you scored!

☐ **Never have I ever walked around the city all night long and came home only in the morning.**

☐ **Never have I ever gone in public without a bra.**

☐ **Never have I ever tasted animal food.**

☐ **Never have I ever worn the same piece of clothing for a week.**

☐ **Never have I ever forged a signature.**

What's your score?_____

5 - Wow! You're amazing!
4 - Not too bad
3 - Meh. Kinda boring
2 - Yikes. Not that great
1 - Time to live a little more!

Sneaky Ass Slice Puzzle 3

This puzzle is fucked up! Can you figure this shit out? Draw each figure in the matching letter and number square below.

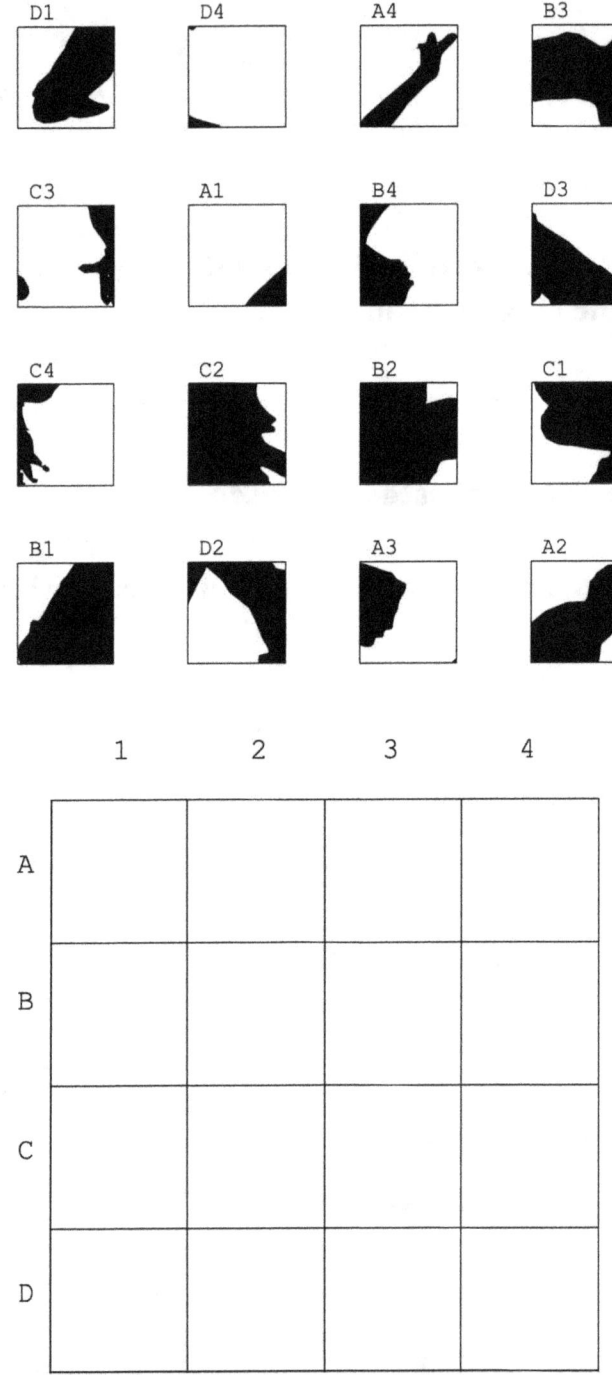

Spot the Damn Difference 2

There are 5 fucking differences in the picture below. Find that shit if you can!

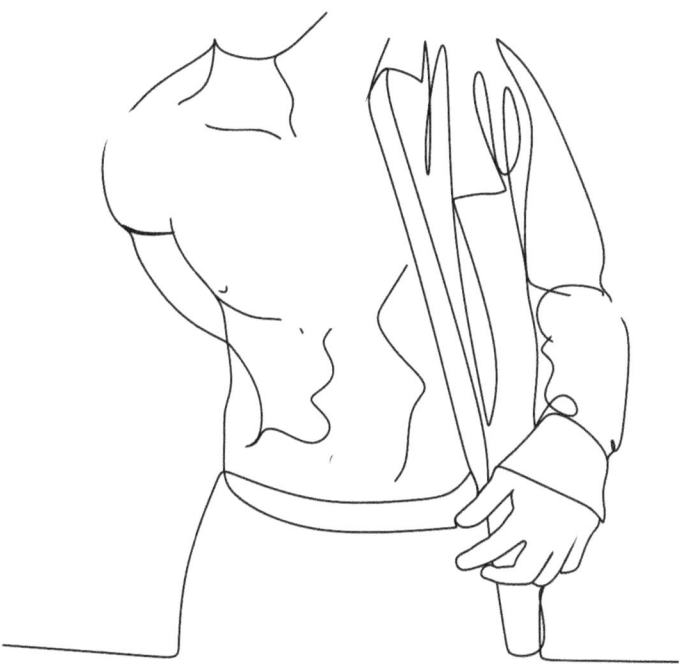

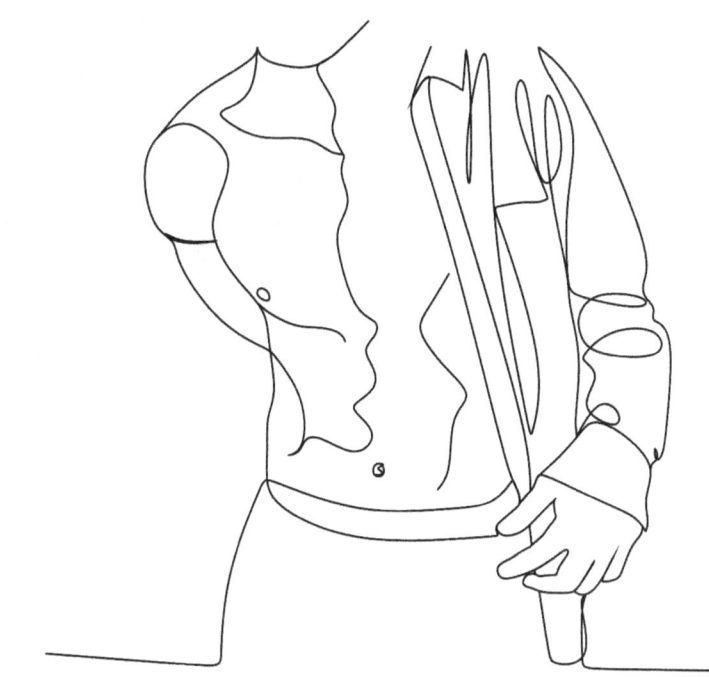

Finish the Fucking Picture 3

Think you know what the fuck this is?
Draw the other half of the picture

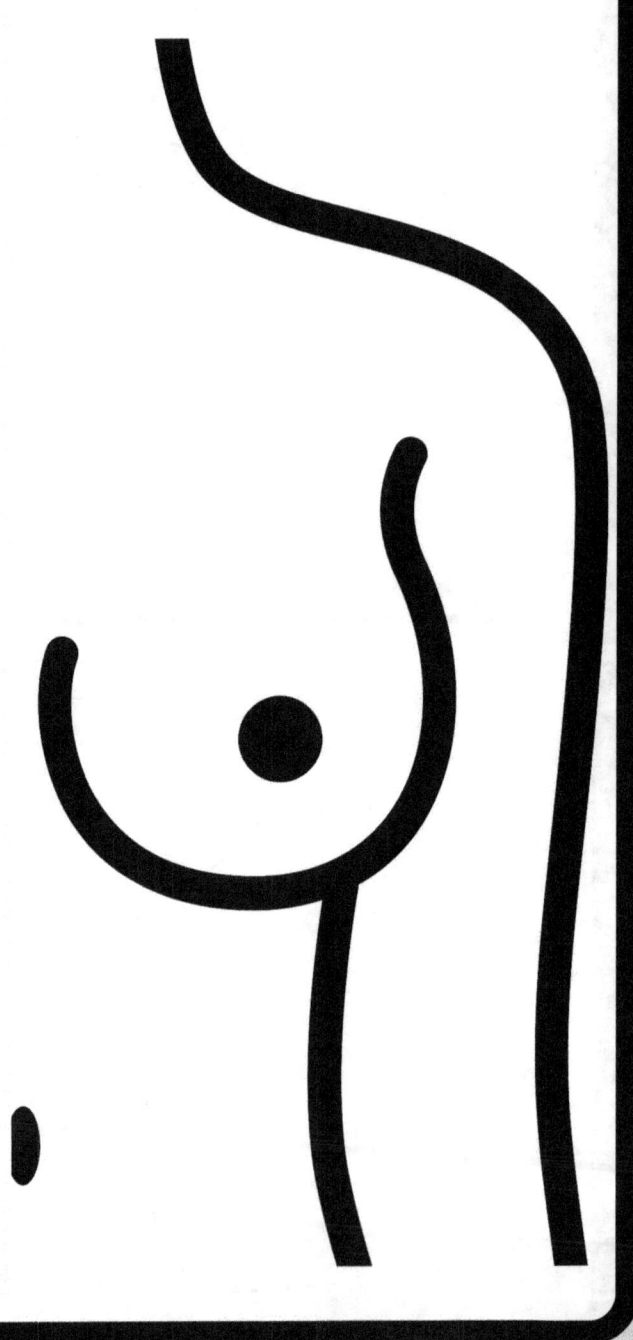

Shitfaced Samurai Sudoku 2

This damn puzzle is hard! I bet you can't figure this damn thing out! Samurai sudoku puzzles consist of five overlapping sudoku grids. The standard sudoku rules apply to each 9 x 9 grid. Place digits from 1 to 9 in each empty cell. Every row, every column, and every 3 x 3 box should contain one of each digit.

Spot the Damn Difference 1

There are 5 fucking differences in the picture below. Find that shit if you can!

Sneaky Ass Slice Puzzle 1

This puzzle is fucked up! Can you figure this shit out? Draw each figure in the matching letter and number square below.

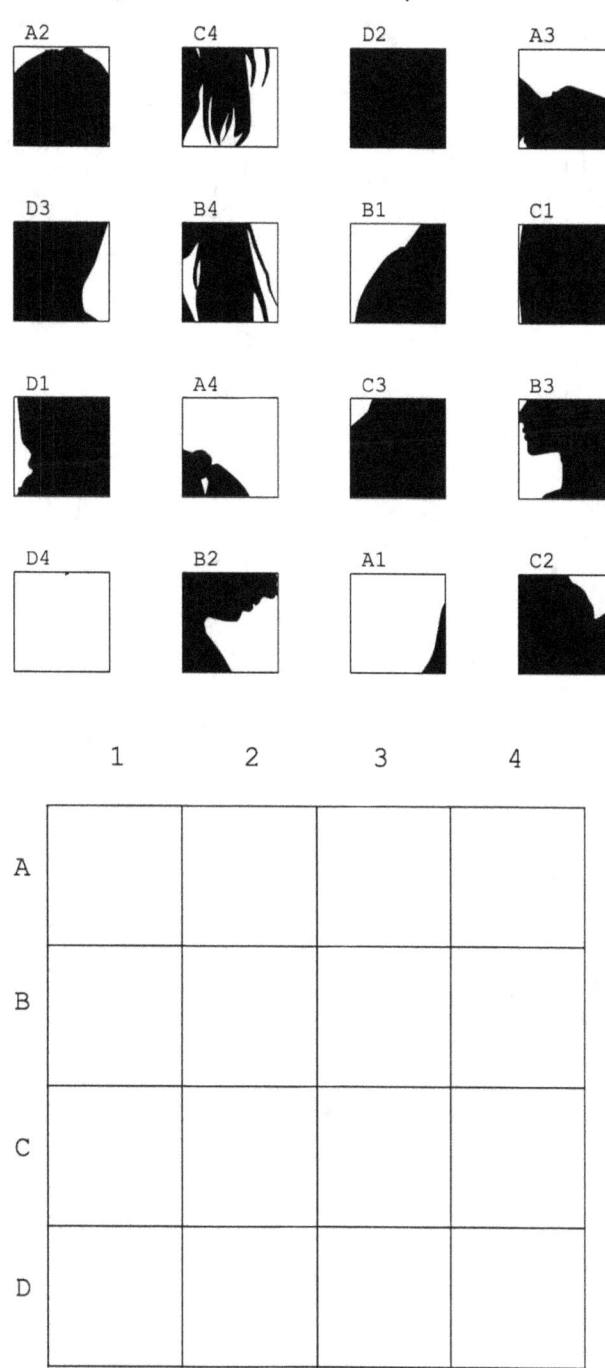

TRUE OR FALSE

53% of American women will not leave the house without makeup on

Circle the answer below

T F

WTF! Word Search 4

Solve this damn puzzle...if you can.

Pissed Off Insults

```
F  R  H  G  P  K  B  S  S  X  E  G  C  T  H
E  U  A  P  U  S  S  Y  P  F  C  M  T  L  M
V  K  C  I  R  P  N  D  B  K  A  V  P  I  Q
Y  F  F  K  S  T  W  A  T  F  F  T  S  K  Q
Y  S  L  B  H  B  W  U  H  M  K  F  G  V  T
T  J  R  Y  I  E  Y  T  I  K  C  U  F  R  T
T  E  G  E  T  T  A  L  I  V  U  C  R  Y  W
L  L  K  I  K  J  C  D  G  S  F  S  Z  P  C
W  B  J  T  I  C  T  H  S  P  F  F  Y  J  B
X  M  G  I  C  Y  U  E  I  R  Z  P  R  F  C
P  B  K  F  K  T  Y  F  T  N  J  Y  B  V  N
I  S  E  I  E  T  P  E  N  U  G  D  B  O  K
U  R  D  C  R  I  S  Y  U  H  O  O  G  W  A
G  Q  Y  C  F  H  B  P  C  K  D  H  V  P  A
J  U  X  Y  Y  S  D  D  Y  P  O  G  P  R  O
```

PRICK	PUSSY	CUNT
SHITTY	TWAT	BITCHING
FUCKFACE	FUCKHEADS	FUCKERS
FUCKITY	SHITKICKER	

OMG **Odd One Out 4**

Okay, this shit is easy! Find the one that's fucking different.

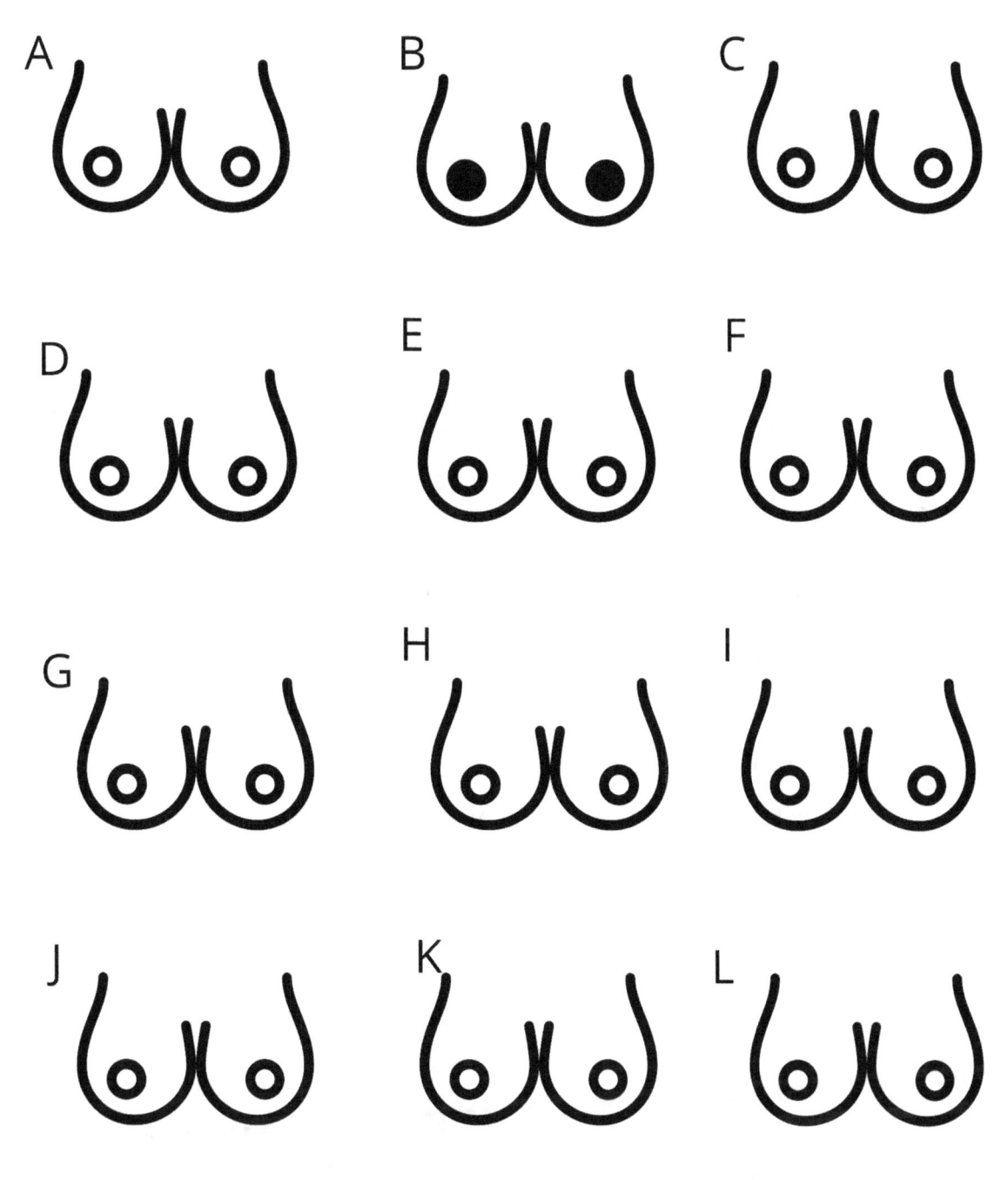

A   B   C

D   E   F

G   H   I

J   K   L

WTH? Word Puzzle 1

British Swear Word Meanings

Are you a smart ass? Think you know all these word meanings. Match this shit up. Write the letter of the correct matching meaning next to each swear word.

1. _____	naff	a. testicles
2. _____	plonker	b. promiscuous woman
3. _____	arse	c. intensifier
4. _____	nutter	d. crazy person
5. _____	bell	e. tasteless, crap
6. _____	pish	f. head of a penis
7. _____	blimey	g. annoying idiot
8. _____	bloody	h. person to be regarded with contempt/envy
9. _____	bollocks	i. riddled with pox; crappy, third-rate
10. _____	bugger	j. variant of ass, acting a fool
11. _____	manky	k. a very unattractive person or thing
12. _____	minger	l. Scottish piss
13. _____	rotter	m. expression of astonishment
14. _____	scrubber	n. worthless, disgusting
15. _____	poxy	o. jerk, silly fool

NEVER HAVE I EVER GAME

How fucking adventurous are you? Check off each item below that you have done. Each checked item is one point. Next add your total points and see how you scored!

- [ ] Never have I ever talked on the phone for longer hours.

- [ ] Never have I ever sent someone "send nudes".

- [ ] Never have I ever been rejected by someone I like.

- [ ] Never have I ever licked food/drinks on someone's body.

- [ ] Never have I ever had to use lubrication.

What's your score?_____

5 - Wow! You're amazing!

4 - Not too bad

3 - Meh. Kinda boring

2 - Yikes. Not that great

1 - Time to live a little more!

WTF! Word Search 5

Solve this damn puzzle...if you can.

A Fucking Bad Day

```
E  A  W  C  O  C  K  S  U  C  K  E  R  B  Y
I  J  I  I  X  G  Q  G  D  D  G  P  M  V  J
T  J  H  A  H  F  R  K  X  X  E  Z  A  C  Z
Q  J  T  B  A  C  U  Q  K  W  Q  P  Z  S  F
L  A  F  U  C  K  I  N  G  T  A  T  N  O  A
F  U  C  K  E  D  D  Y  T  I  H  S  C  L  E
A  U  C  T  C  Y  P  K  C  O  C  P  N  C  L
D  V  X  B  C  F  U  C  K  S  V  I  L  L  E
E  B  S  H  S  N  D  R  B  L  U  N  A  H  K
B  R  E  K  C  U  F  R  E  H  T  O  M  Y  E
I  V  T  B  U  L  L  S  H  I  T  D  J  S  F
T  H  O  U  D  L  K  F  C  Q  Z  G  Z  U  L
C  U  R  S  T  I  U  D  I  C  K  Y  E  I  C
H  A  X  K  A  C  Y  W  I  T  R  N  K  I  I
V  T  R  M  K  U  I  P  A  O  J  Z  B  V  U
```

FUCKING	FUCK	SHIT
MOTHERFUCKER	FUCKED	DICK
BITCH	BULLSHIT	COCK
COCKSUCKER	FUCKSVILLE	

Kickass Kakuro 2

The rules of Kakuro are fucking simple - place the damn numbers 1 to 9 into the puzzle grid so that each continuous horizontal or vertical run of empty squares adds up to the value to the left of it or above it respectively. This value is shown either to the right or below a diagonal line. Got it? Now go and solve this shit!

Motherfucking Maze 2

Try to solve this hard ass maze! Start from the top and figure out how to get the fuck out of this shit!

WTF! Word Search 6

Solve this damn puzzle...if you can.

Sweary Phrases

```
O D Q H G P A O H J N T X E Z H V L K R
X C K P Y D G L E U P V E T S E X Y O T
W N K D Y O Q S K M V C S L T A C Z C A
M J A Q Z G G W S P M D B Z A V H C F H
M S Q Z C G S L H I G M F K H E J F E N
W L L Y E O L E U N Y Y E X W N D O L S
G D F K H N Z B T J O Z F J E S Y R I J
Z L C V V I M S T E A S X Z H T U O V F
O U G G R T D J H H U T B J T O P H E F
S N K O Y E V B E O Z I Q R T B G P D B
O Z W O E Z K A F S E R G X A E Q Q E N
T C G D H D Q C R H R G F A H T V K H U
I A A G E N D Z O A S Y A N W S J F T M
B N W R H O M G N P S M Q D S Y F W T W
B V M I T K R Q T H T S I D S U Y A A F
A H P E T L H O D A B S E H P E B T H N
N S E F A S Z A O T A I Q A A R Q I W Q
G M E H H Y W G O Z V K S B G J L G T L
A B E M W Y R X R Z U Y E K R A L A M H
D A K Z U E L O H E I P R U O Y T U H S
```

KISS MY GRITS	SHUT YOUR PIEHOLE	JUMPIN JEHOSHAPHAT
WHAT THE DEVIL	SHUT THE FRONT DOOR	SUCK EGGS
HEAVENS TO BETSY	WHAT THE WHAT	GOOD GRIEF
MALARKEY	WHAT THE HEY	DOG GONIT
DAGNABBIT		

Crazy Ass Cryptogram 2

What the fuck is this? Can you solve the shit out of this puzzle? Find the correct letters that correspond to the letters shown below to solve the secret phrase.

A	B	C	D	E	F	G	H	I	J	K	L	M	N	O	P	Q	R	S	T	U	V	W	X	Y	Z
24	17	1	4	14	2	3	5	8	22	16	26	7	13	18	19	20	10	15	25	6	9	12	11	21	23

__ __ __   __ __ __ __   __ __ __ __ __ __ __   __ __
25 5 14   17 14 15 25   10 14 9 14 13 3 14   8 15

__ __ __ __ __ __ __   __ __ __ __ __ __ __
7 24 15 15 8 9 14   15 6 1 1 14 15 15

OMG **Odd One Out 4**

Damn this shit is hard! Try to find the one that's fucking different.

A

B

C

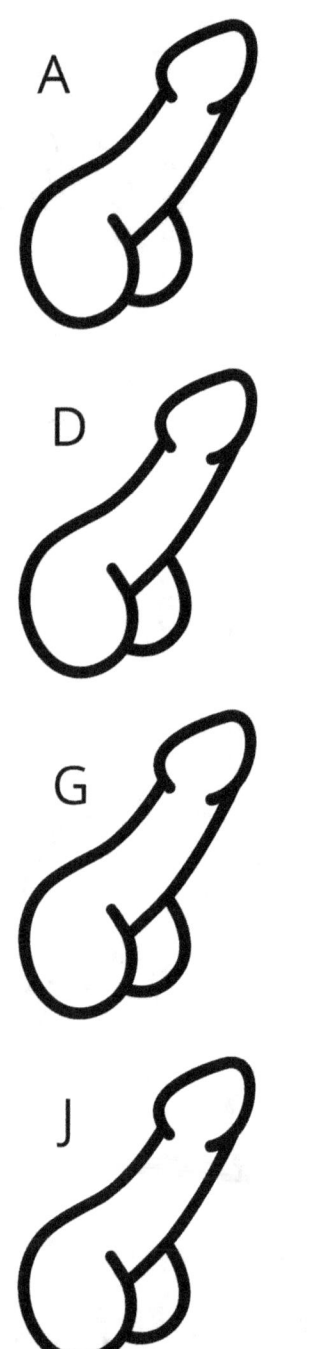
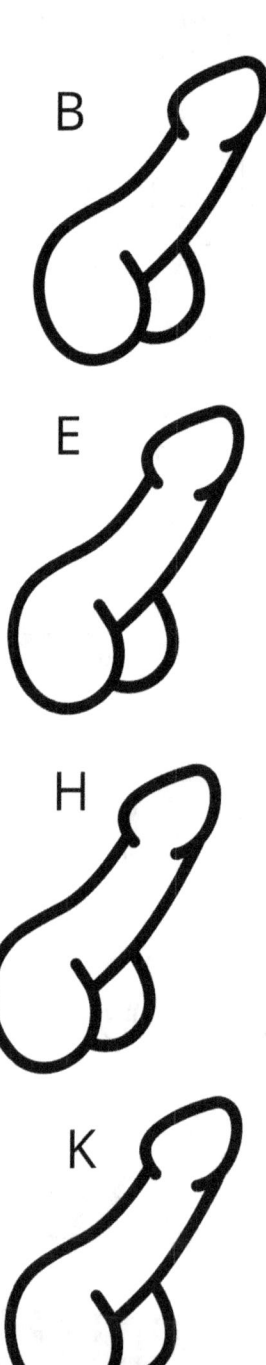
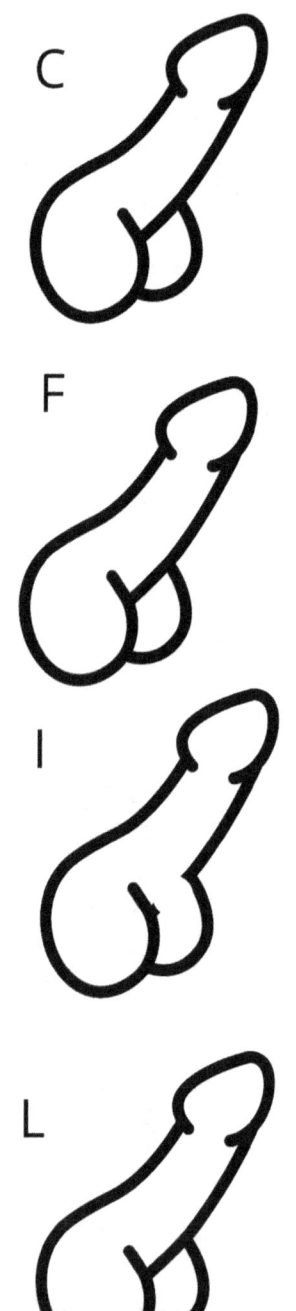

D

E

F

G

H

I

J

K

L

NEVER HAVE I EVER GAME

How fucking adventurous are you? Check off each item below that you have done. Each checked item is one point. Next add your total points and see how you scored!

☐ Never have I ever stalked someone I liked on social media.

☐ Never have I ever pretended to not receive someone's text just because I didn't want to reply.

☐ Never have I ever cleared my phone or computer history.

☐ Never have I ever had a lie backfire right in front of my eyes.

☐ Never have I ever pretended to be sick so I could get out of something?

What's your score? _____

5 - Wow! You're amazing!
4 - Not too bad
3 - Meh. Kinda boring
2 - Yikes. Not that great
1 - Time to live a little more!

Cocky Crossword 2

Solve this shit ...if you can.

Shit Happens

ACROSS
1 human fecal matter. They are the lowest of the low.
6 To accomplish something by brute force, without planning, elegance, or rework.
7 grin given by the grinner to show or perhaps hide an inside thought
8 Someone who enters a fast food establishment for the sole purpose of using their public restroom
9 A complete dumbass; a genuine moron
10 An 'ebonic' expression for an extremely curvaceous female behind
11 When chaos arrives; when something pops off; If you can't take anymore
12 Many, as in, more than a few in quantity.

DOWN
2 When you sit on the toilet and fart.
3 To be completely and honestly serious.
4 When something happens that is out of one's control and usually results in a negative situations
5 Someone who is the epitome of scum, The lowest of the low.

Kickass Kakuro 3

The rules of Kakuro are fucking simple - place the damn numbers 1 to 9 into the puzzle grid so that each continuous horizontal or vertical run of empty squares adds up to the value to the left of it or above it respectively. This value is shown either to the right or below a diagonal line. Got it? Now go and solve this shit!

 **! WTH? Word Puzzle 2**
Swear Word Meanings

Are you a smart ass? Think you know all these word meanings. Match this shit up. Write the letter of the correct matching meaning next to each swear word.

1.	bastard	a.	moron
2.	bitch	b.	vaginal fart
3.	dookie	c.	poop
4.	douchebag	d.	male genitalia
5.	dipshit	e.	male genitalia
6.	fuckoff	f.	loser
7.	fucktard	g.	worst
8.	lameass	h.	female dog
9.	lardass	i.	female personal hygiene product
10.	nutsack	j.	overweight lazy person
11.	schlong	k.	idiot
12.	queef	l.	illegitimate child
13.	shitfaced	m.	drunk
14.	shittiest	n.	dirty girl
15.	skank	o.	go away
16.	slut	p.	sexually popular woman

Sexy Sudoku 6

*Damn this shit is hard! Try to kick
this puzzles ass before it kicks yours!*

	9						8	
2		5	6		8	7		9
	7	8		9		1	6	
	2		4	5	7		9	
		6	2		1	3		
	5		9	6	3		1	
	3	2		4		5	7	
5		4	7		6	9		1
	6						2	

Motherfucking Maze 4

Try to solve this hard ass maze! Start from the top and figure out how to get the fuck out of this shit!

TRUE OR FALSE

According to the World Health Organization more than 114 million acts of sex are performed each day around the world.

Circle the answer below

T   F

Shitfaced Samurai Sudoku 1

This damn puzzle is hard! I bet you can't figure this damn thing out! Samurai sudoku puzzles consist of five overlapping sudoku grids. The standard sudoku rules apply to each 9 x 9 grid. Place digits from 1 to 9 in each empty cell. Every row, every column, and every 3 x 3 box should contain one of each digit.

Sneaky Ass Slice Puzzle 2

This puzzle is fucked up! Can you figure this shit out? Draw each figure in the matching letter and number square below.

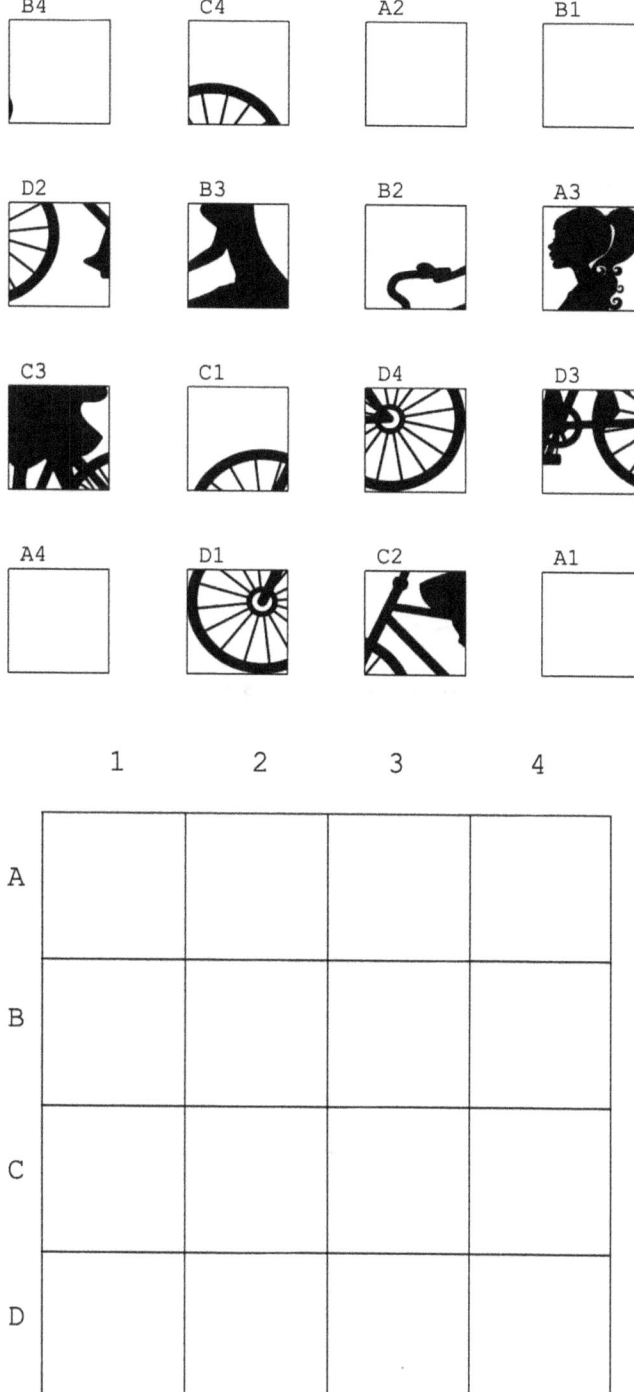

Spot the Damn Difference 4

There are 5 fucking differences in the picture below. Find that shit if you can!

Puzzle
Solutions

1

7	6	9	2	3	4	1	8	5
3	4	5	7	1	8	2	6	9
2	8	1	6	9	5	3	4	7
9	7	2	3	8	1	4	5	6
4	5	3	9	7	6	8	1	2
6	1	8	5	4	2	9	7	3
1	3	6	4	2	7	5	9	8
5	2	4	8	6	9	7	3	1
8	9	7	1	5	3	6	2	4

2

8	5	3	6	7	1	9	2	4
6	2	1	8	4	9	7	3	5
4	9	7	5	2	3	8	6	1
5	3	4	9	1	7	6	8	2
2	8	9	3	6	4	1	5	7
7	1	6	2	5	8	3	4	9
1	6	2	7	8	5	4	9	3
3	4	5	1	9	6	2	7	8
9	7	8	4	3	2	5	1	6

3

4	6	1	7	3	5	9	8	2
2	7	9	4	6	8	3	5	1
5	8	3	2	1	9	6	7	4
6	2	8	5	4	1	7	9	3
7	1	5	3	9	2	4	6	8
3	9	4	8	7	6	2	1	5
8	3	2	6	5	7	1	4	9
1	5	6	9	2	4	8	3	7
9	4	7	1	8	3	5	2	6

4

1	8	7	6	3	9	2	5	4
3	2	6	4	1	5	8	9	7
5	9	4	7	8	2	6	3	1
4	3	1	5	7	8	9	6	2
7	6	9	1	2	3	5	4	8
2	5	8	9	6	4	7	1	3
6	7	5	8	4	1	3	2	9
8	4	2	3	9	6	1	7	5
9	1	3	2	5	7	4	8	6

5

5	2	9	6	1	3	4	8	7
1	4	8	9	2	7	6	3	5
3	7	6	5	4	8	1	9	2
4	9	2	3	6	1	5	7	8
8	3	7	2	5	4	9	6	1
6	1	5	8	7	9	3	2	4
7	8	1	4	3	6	2	5	9
9	5	3	1	8	2	7	4	6
2	6	4	7	9	5	8	1	3

6

6	9	3	1	7	4	2	8	5
2	1	5	6	3	8	7	4	9
4	7	8	5	9	2	1	6	3
3	2	1	4	5	7	6	9	8
9	4	6	2	8	1	3	5	7
8	5	7	9	6	3	4	1	2
1	3	2	8	4	9	5	7	6
5	8	4	7	2	6	9	3	1
7	6	9	3	1	5	8	2	4

British Swear Word Meanings

Write the letter of the correct matching meaning next to each swear word.

1.	e	naff	a. testicles
2.	g	plonker	b. promiscuous woman
3.	j	arse	c. intensifier
4.	d	nutter	d. crazy person
5.	f	bell	e. tasteless, crap
6.	l	pish	f. head of a penis
7.	m	blimey	g. annoying idiot
8.	c	bloody	h. person to be regarded with contempt/envy
9.	a	bollocks	i. riddled with pox; crappy, third-rate
10.	o	bugger	j. variant of ass, acting a fool
11.	n	manky	k. a very unattractive person or thing
12.	k	minger	l. Scottish piss
13.	h	rotter	m. expression of astonishment
14.	b	scrubber	n. worthless, disgusting
15.	i	poxy	o. jerk, silly fool

Swear Word Meanings

Write the letter of the correct matching meaning next to each swear word.

1.	l	bastard	a. moron
2.	h	bitch	b. vaginal fart
3.	c	dookie	c. poop
4.	i	douchebag	d. male genitalia
5.	k	dipshit	e. male genitalia
6.	o	fuckoff	f. loser
7.	a	fucktard	g. worst
8.	f	lameass	h. female dog
9.	j	lardass	i. female personal hygiene product
10.	e	nutsack	j. overweight lazy person
11.	d	schlong	k. idiot
12.	b	queef	l. illegitimate child
13.	m	shitfaced	m. drunk
14.	g	shittiest	n. dirty girl
15.	n	skank	o. go away
16.	p	slut	p. sexually popular woman

Random Fuckery

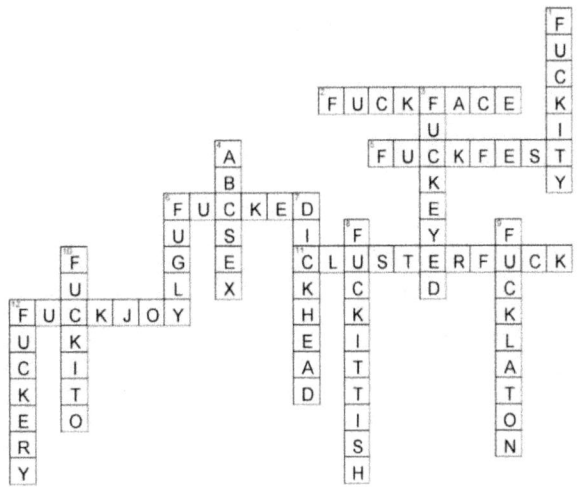

Penis

Shit Happens

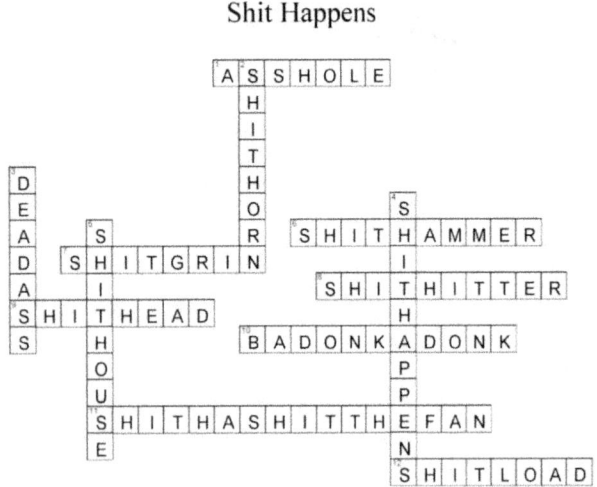

Middle Finger

Top 20 Popular British Swear Words

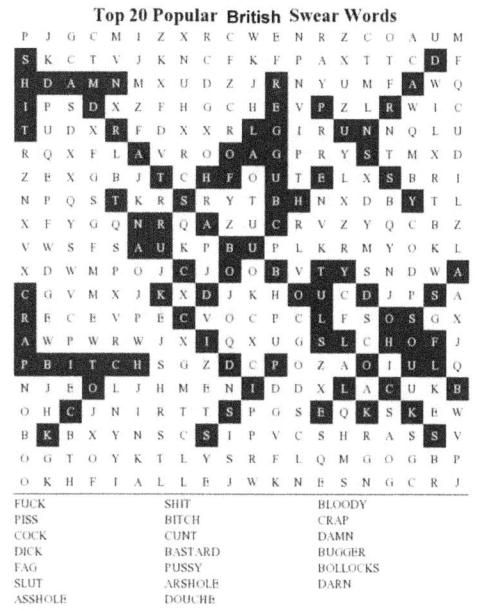

FUCK	SHIT	BLOODY
PISS	BITCH	CRAP
COCK	CUNT	DAMN
DICK	BASTARD	BUGGER
FAG	PUSSY	BOLLOCKS
SLUT	ARSHOLE	DARN
ASSHOLE	DOUCHE	

Top 15 Southern Swear Words

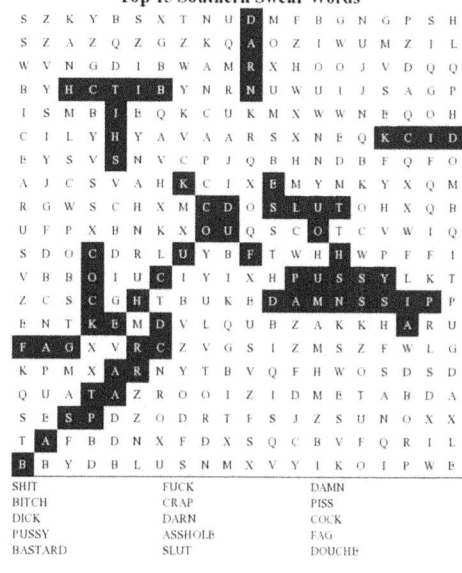

SHIT	FUCK	DAMN
BITCH	CRAP	PISS
DICK	DARN	COCK
PUSSY	ASSHOLE	FAG
BASTARD	SLUT	DOUCHE

Feelin' Shitty

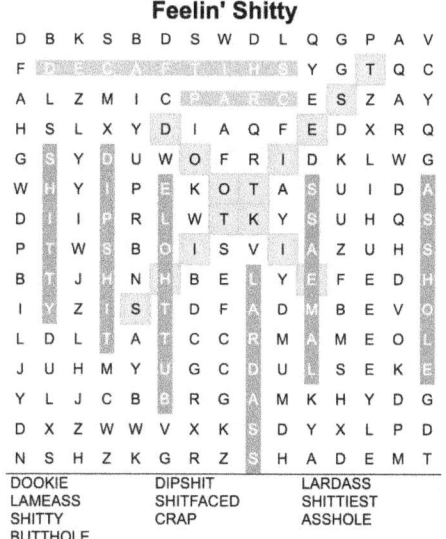

DOOKIE	DIPSHIT	LARDASS
LAMEASS	SHITFACED	SHITTIEST
SHITTY	CRAP	ASSHOLE
BUTTHOLE		

Kinda Sweary

BITEME	PISSOFF	JERK
BUTTHOLE	BULLCRAP	DARN
IT	BLUEBALLS	DOUCHEBAG
CRAPPER	SHOOT	

Sweary Phrases

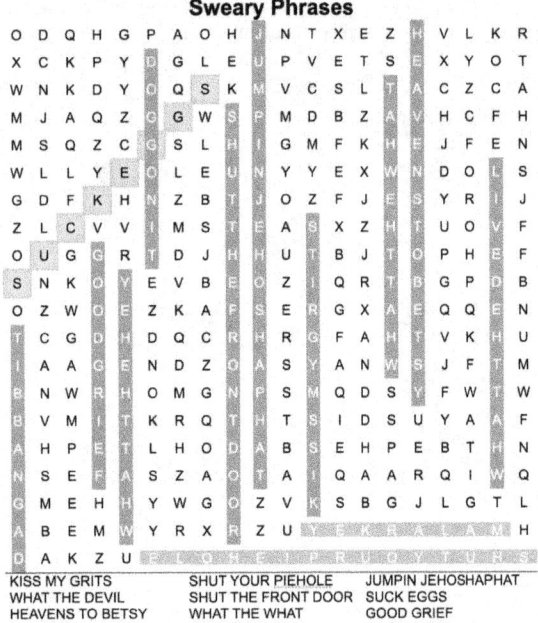

KISS MY GRITS
WHAT THE DEVIL
HEAVENS TO BETSY
MALARKEY
DAGNABBIT

SHUT YOUR PIEHOLE
SHUT THE FRONT DOOR
WHAT THE WHAT
WHAT THE HEY

JUMPIN JEHOSHAPHAT
SUCK EGGS
GOOD GRIEF
DOG GONIT

A Fucking Bad Day

FUCKING
MOTHERFUCKER
BITCH
COCKSUCKER

FUCK
FUCKED
BULLSHIT
FUCKSVILLE

SHIT
DICK
COCK

Pissed Off Insults

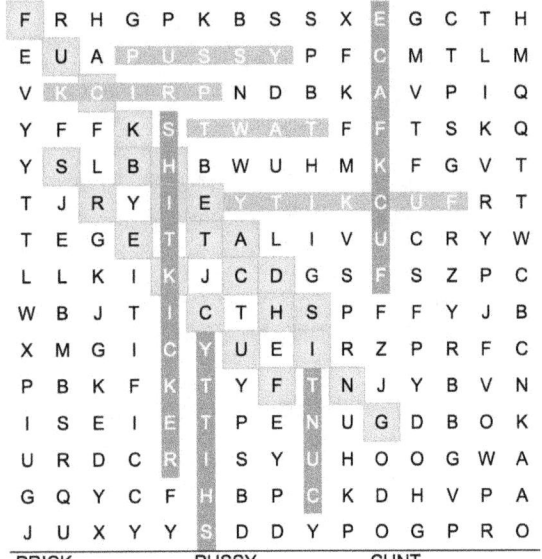

PRICK
SHITTY
FUCKFACE
FUCKITY

PUSSY
TWAT
FUCKHEADS
SHITKICKER

CUNT
BITCHING
FUCKERS

Cryptograms

A	B	C	D	E	F	G	H	I	J	K	L	M	N	O	P	Q	R	S	T	U	V	W	X	Y	Z
13	7	20	19	6	16	25	23	9	1	4	15	21	8	17	12	2	5	14	26	22	10	11	24	18

```
I   TOOK   THE   ROAD   LESS
3   14 8 8 1   14 23 6   2 8 13 19   4 6 5 5

TRAVELLED   NOW   I   DON'T   KNOW
14 2 13 22 6 4 4 6 19   21 8 10   3   19 8 21   14   1 21 8 10

WHERE   THE   FUCK   I   AM
10 23 6 2 6   14 23 6   16 26 20 1   3   13 15
```

A	B	C	D	E	F	G	H	I	J	K	L	M	N	O	P	Q	R	S	T	U	V	W	X	Y	Z
24	17	1	4	14	2	3	5	8	22	16	26	7	13	18	19	20	10	15	25	6	9	12	11	21	23

```
THE   BEST   REVENGE   IS
25 5 14   17 14 15 25   10 14 9 14 13 3 14   8 15

MASSIVE   SUCCESS
7 24 15 15 8 9 14   15 6 1 1 14 15 15
```

Maze puzzles

Maze puzzle 3

Maze puzzle 4

Slice Puzzle 1

Slice Puzzle 2

Slice Puzzle 3

Finish the picture 1

Finish the picture 2

Finish the picture 2

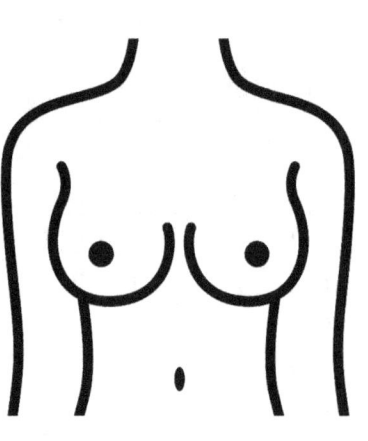

Spot the difference

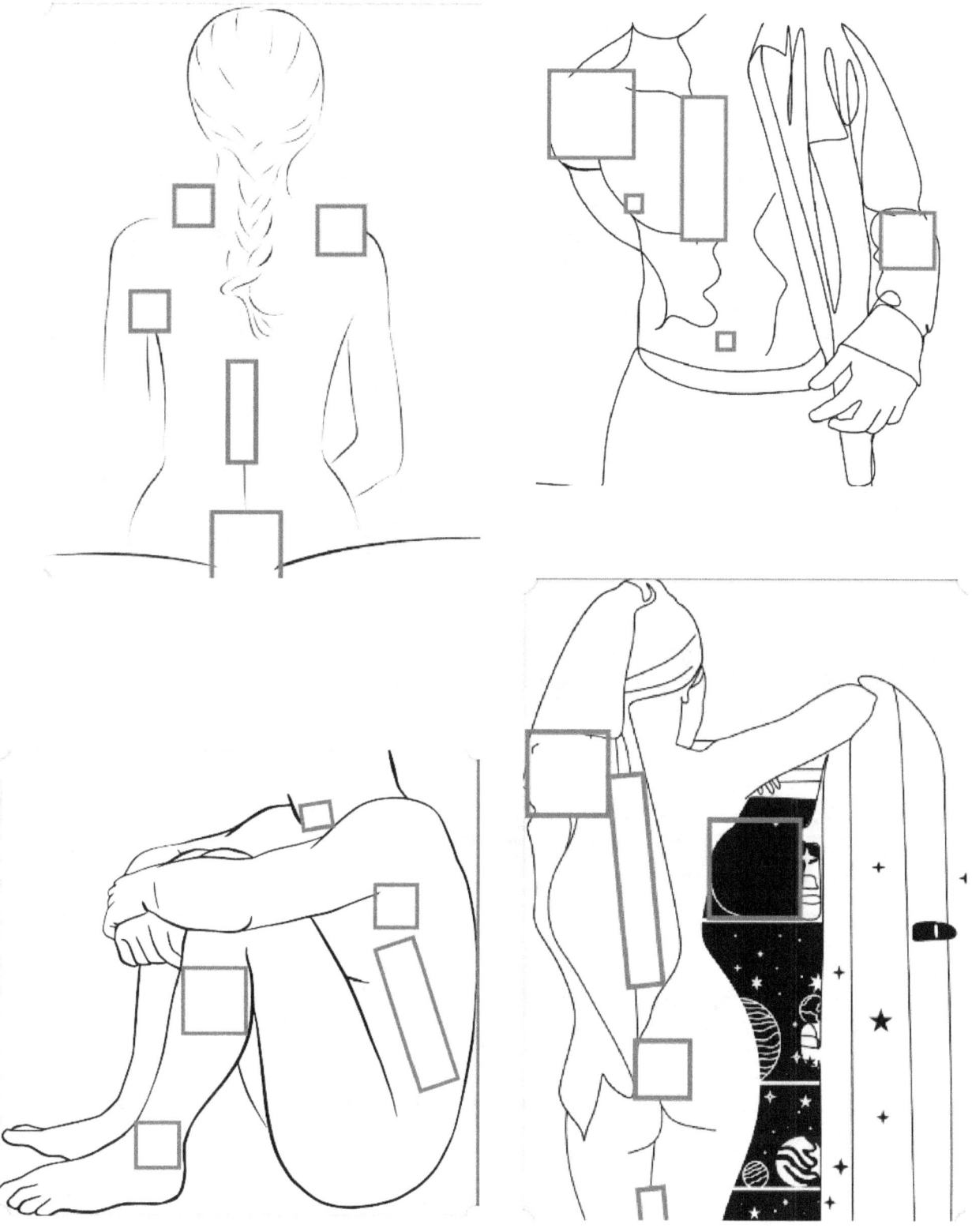

Odd One Out

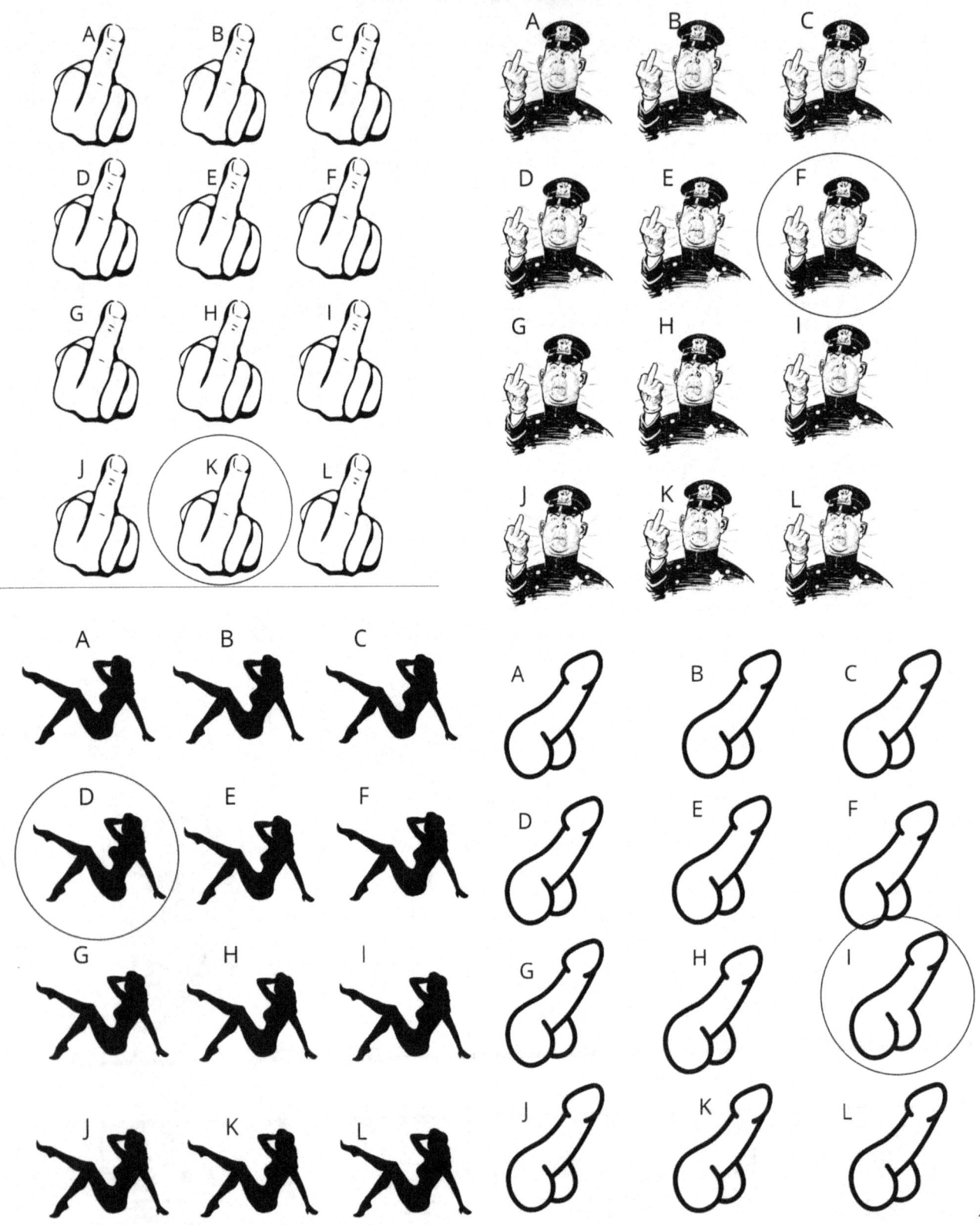

Word scramble

1. dnar — darn

2. rpca — crap

3. bllu — bull

4. npku — punk

5. eby leiafic — bye felicia

6. sith uskcs — this sucks

7. ibet em — bite me

8. ejrk — jerk

9. god gneo it — dog gone it

10. ckrpi — prick

11. sblal — balls

12. uttblheo — butthole

13. sips — piss

14. uodceh — douche

Odd One Out

True or False

A pig's penis is shaped like a corkscrew. **TRUE.**

Married men revealed that they change their underwear twice as often as single men. **TRUE.**

48 percent of the content on the internet is pornographic. **FALSE.**

53% of American women will not leave the house without makeup on. **TRUE.**

More than 114 million acts of sex are performed each day around the world. (World Health Organization) **TRUE.**

Samarai Sudoku 1

```
1 7 3 4 8 5 9 6 2     8 9 2 6 3 1 4 7 5
8 4 5 2 9 6 1 3 7     4 6 1 7 8 5 2 9 3
2 9 6 1 3 7 5 4 8     5 7 3 2 9 4 8 6 1
5 2 9 6 7 4 8 1 3     7 8 9 4 1 2 3 5 6
6 8 4 9 1 3 7 2 5     3 2 5 8 7 6 1 4 9
3 1 7 5 2 8 6 9 4     6 1 4 9 5 3 7 8 2
4 5 2 7 6 1 3 8 9  6 2 5  1 4 7 3 6 9 5 2 8
9 6 8 3 5 2 4 7 1  9 8 3  2 5 6 1 4 8 9 3 7
7 3 1 8 4 9 2 5 6  7 1 4  9 3 8 5 2 7 6 1 4
                   1 4 5 2 6 7 8 9 3
                   6 9 7 3 5 8 4 2 1
                   8 2 3 4 9 1 7 6 5
9 6 2 1 7 8 5 3 4  1 7 2  6 8 9 3 7 5 2 1 4
1 3 5 9 4 2 7 6 8  5 4 9  3 1 2 6 4 8 5 9 7
7 4 8 3 5 6 9 1 2  8 3 6  5 7 4 2 1 9 6 3 8
4 2 3 8 9 5 1 7 6     1 6 8 9 5 7 4 2 3
5 8 7 6 1 3 2 4 9     7 9 3 4 8 2 1 6 5
6 1 9 4 2 7 3 8 5     2 4 5 1 6 3 7 8 9
3 7 6 5 8 9 4 2 1     4 5 1 8 9 6 3 7 2
8 9 1 2 3 4 6 5 7     8 3 7 5 2 1 9 4 6
2 5 4 7 6 1 8 9 3     9 2 6 7 3 4 8 5 1
```

Samarai Sudoku 2

```
8 4 5 3 9 2 7 1 6     1 9 4 8 7 3 6 2 5
9 6 3 5 7 1 2 8 4     8 7 3 2 5 6 1 9 4
7 1 2 4 6 8 9 3 5     6 5 2 9 4 1 3 8 7
1 2 8 9 4 5 6 7 3     3 4 7 5 1 9 2 6 8
5 9 7 6 8 3 4 2 1     5 2 1 7 6 8 9 4 3
6 3 4 1 2 7 5 9 8     9 6 8 4 3 2 7 5 1
4 7 9 8 3 6 1 5 2  3 4 6  7 8 9 3 2 4 5 1 6
2 8 1 7 5 4 3 6 9  7 8 2  4 1 5 6 9 7 8 3 2
3 5 6 2 1 9 8 4 7  1 9 5  2 3 6 1 8 5 4 7 9
                   4 2 1 6 7 3 9 5 8
                   6 7 8 5 2 9 1 4 3
                   9 3 5 8 1 4 6 7 2
7 3 4 5 1 9 2 8 6  4 5 1  3 9 7 5 1 2 8 4 6
9 2 8 6 7 4 5 1 3  9 6 7  8 2 4 9 6 7 1 5 3
5 1 6 3 8 2 7 9 4  2 3 8  5 6 1 4 3 8 9 7 2
3 5 1 2 9 7 4 6 8     6 3 8 7 5 1 4 2 9
8 9 2 4 6 3 1 7 5     7 4 9 8 2 3 6 1 5
6 4 7 1 5 8 3 2 9     2 1 5 6 9 4 7 3 8
1 6 3 8 2 5 9 4 7     9 7 2 1 8 5 3 6 4
4 8 9 7 3 1 6 5 2     1 8 3 2 4 6 5 9 7
2 7 5 9 4 6 8 3 1     4 5 6 3 7 9 2 8 1
```

Samarai Sudoku 3

```
7 4 9 5 8 2 6 3 1     8 7 6 5 2 4 3 9 1
8 3 1 7 4 6 5 2 9     9 1 3 6 7 8 4 2 5
6 5 2 3 1 9 7 8 4     2 4 5 1 3 9 6 7 8
3 6 4 2 5 1 8 9 7     1 5 4 7 8 2 9 3 6
2 1 8 9 7 4 3 5 6     3 6 9 4 5 1 7 8 2
9 7 5 6 3 8 1 4 2     7 8 2 3 9 6 1 5 4
4 9 3 1 6 5 2 7 8  4 3 6  5 9 1 8 4 3 2 6 7
1 8 7 4 2 3 9 6 5  1 2 7  4 3 8 2 6 7 5 1 9
5 2 6 8 9 7 4 1 3  5 8 9  6 2 7 9 1 5 8 4 3
                   3 9 6 7 1 8 2 5 4
                   5 8 4 3 6 2 1 7 9
                   1 2 7 9 4 5 8 6 3
3 7 9 2 8 5 6 4 1  2 7 3  9 8 5 2 6 3 4 7 1
1 8 4 3 6 9 7 5 2  8 9 4  3 1 6 5 4 7 8 9 2
6 5 2 4 7 1 8 3 9  6 5 1  7 4 2 1 9 8 6 3 5
5 1 6 8 4 2 3 9 7     1 3 4 9 8 5 2 6 7
2 3 7 5 9 6 4 1 8     8 6 9 7 2 1 3 5 4
9 4 8 7 1 3 5 2 6     5 2 7 4 3 6 9 1 8
8 9 1 6 5 4 2 7 3     2 7 3 6 1 4 5 8 9
4 6 3 1 2 7 9 8 5     6 9 1 8 5 2 7 4 3
7 2 5 9 3 8 1 6 4     4 5 8 3 7 9 1 2 6
```

Kakuro 1

	16\	14\			11\	4\
\12	7	5		\12	9	3
\10	9	1	\19 12\	9	2	1
	\12	8	1	3	16\	
		\17	4	7	6	3\
4\ 16\	1	9	6	4\	3	1
\11	3	8		\9	7	2

Kakuro 2

	16\	15\			3\	17\
16\	7	9		\9	1	8
14\	9	5	18\ 15\	4	2	9
	\8	1	2	5	20\	
	\20	8	9	3	8\	
3\ 9\	2	5	1	\12	9	3
\5	1	4		\13	8	5

Kakuro 3

	6\	16\			15\	12\
3\	2	1		16\	9	7
10\	4	6	20\ 14\	3	6	5
	\24	9	7	8	15\	
		\19	6	9	4	4\
8\ 7\	2	4	1	10\	9	1
\9	6	3		\5	2	3

Thank you for purchasing this book! Did you enjoy the "Never Would I Ever" questions? We want you to keep having fun, so as a special thank you please download this FREE gift:

201 Never Would I Ever questions for ages 18 and over!

The questions come in a pdf that you can download to your phone and easily take with you on your next trip, enjoy alone, or with your friends!

Download here:
https://linktr.ee/snarkygirlz

If you enjoyed this book please consider leaving a review online. Your feedback helps us make more and better books for you.

Thank you!